50 British Tea-Time Treats

By: Kelly Johnson

Table of Contents

- Arequipe
- Pandebono
- Almojábanas
- Empanadas
- Arepas
- Bocadillo
- Buñuelos
- Pan de yuca
- Pan de bono de queso
- Obleas
- Galletas de anís
- Galletas de maíz
- Torta de aceite
- Torta de queso
- Cuca
- Bizcochos
- Torta de naranja
- Roscones
- Pan de leche
- Postre de natas
- Tamales
- Churros
- Torta de chocolate
- Galletas de coco
- Merengones
- Chocoramo
- Pionono
- Cocadas
- Masarepa con queso
- Pasteles de carne
- Canelazos
- Empanaditas de dulce
- Torta de arándano
- Galletas de guanabana
- Pan de piña

- Bizcocho de tres leches
- Arroz con leche
- Panqueques con arequipe
- Ajiaco (served with bread)
- Pan relleno de dulce
- Pargo frito con yuca
- Torta de maíz
- Mazamorra
- Dulce de leche
- Bocaditos de guanábana
- Torta de remolacha
- Suspiros
- Pan de zapallo
- Pudding de aguacate
- Brevas con arequipe

Arequipe (Dulce de Leche)

Ingredients:

- 4 cups (1 liter) whole milk
- 1 1/4 cups (250g) granulated sugar
- 1/2 tsp baking soda
- 1/4 tsp vanilla extract (optional)

Instructions:

1. In a heavy-bottomed saucepan, combine milk, sugar, and baking soda.
2. Bring the mixture to a boil over medium heat, stirring constantly to prevent burning.
3. Lower the heat and continue to cook, stirring frequently, for 1.5-2 hours, until the mixture thickens and turns a caramel color.
4. Stir in vanilla extract, if using.
5. Remove from heat and allow to cool slightly before transferring to jars. Let it cool completely before storing.

Pandebono

Ingredients:

- 2 cups (250g) tapioca flour
- 1 cup (125g) grated cheese (such as queso fresco or mozzarella)
- 1/2 cup (120ml) milk
- 1/2 cup (115g) unsalted butter, softened
- 1 large egg
- 1 tsp baking powder
- 1/4 tsp salt

Instructions:

1. Preheat oven to 375°F (190°C) and line a baking sheet with parchment paper.
2. In a bowl, combine tapioca flour, baking powder, and salt.
3. In another bowl, mix cheese, milk, butter, and egg until smooth.
4. Gradually mix in dry ingredients, kneading the dough until it forms a smooth ball.
5. Shape the dough into small balls and place them on the baking sheet.
6. Bake for 12-15 minutes, or until golden brown.

Almojábanas

Ingredients:

- 2 cups (250g) tapioca flour
- 1 cup (125g) grated cheese (preferably a mix of mozzarella and queso fresco)
- 1/2 cup (120ml) milk
- 1/2 cup (115g) unsalted butter, softened
- 2 large eggs
- 1 tsp baking powder
- 1/4 tsp salt

Instructions:

1. Preheat oven to 375°F (190°C) and line a baking sheet with parchment paper.
2. In a bowl, combine tapioca flour, baking powder, and salt.
3. In another bowl, beat eggs, milk, butter, and cheese until smooth.
4. Gradually stir in the dry ingredients and mix until dough forms.
5. Shape dough into small rounds and place them on the baking sheet.
6. Bake for 12-15 minutes until golden and puffed.

Empanadas

Ingredients:

For the dough:

- 2 1/2 cups (310g) all-purpose flour
- 1/2 tsp salt
- 1/2 cup (120g) unsalted butter, chilled and cubed
- 1 egg
- 1/4 cup (60ml) water

For the filling:

- 1 lb (450g) ground beef or chicken, cooked
- 1 small onion, chopped
- 1/2 cup (75g) diced potatoes (optional)
- 1/4 cup (60ml) tomato sauce
- 1/4 tsp cumin
- 1/4 tsp paprika
- Salt and pepper to taste

Instructions:

1. For the dough: In a bowl, mix flour and salt. Add butter and rub into the flour until crumbly.
2. Add egg and water and mix until dough forms. Cover and refrigerate for 30 minutes.
3. For the filling: Cook ground meat with onions and spices. Add tomato sauce and potatoes, if using, and cook until well combined. Let cool.
4. Roll out the dough, cut into circles, and spoon the filling into the center. Fold over and seal the edges.
5. Fry in hot oil for 3-4 minutes until golden, or bake at 375°F (190°C) for 20 minutes.

Arepas

Ingredients:

- 2 cups (250g) arepa flour (masarepa)
- 2 1/2 cups (600ml) water
- 1 tsp salt
- 1 tbsp vegetable oil

Instructions:

1. In a large bowl, combine arepa flour and salt. Slowly add water, mixing with your hands until the dough is smooth and soft.
2. Divide the dough into small balls and flatten them into discs.
3. Heat oil in a pan over medium heat and cook the arepas for 5-7 minutes per side, until golden brown.

Bocadillo

Ingredients:

- 1 lb (450g) guava paste, sliced
- 1/2 cup (120g) sugar (optional, if needed)

Instructions:

1. Slice guava paste into thin pieces.
2. If using, melt sugar in a saucepan with a small amount of water to create a syrup.
3. Spread the guava slices on a plate and drizzle with syrup, if desired.
4. Serve as a sweet snack or as part of a cheese platter.

Buñuelos

Ingredients:

- 2 cups (250g) all-purpose flour
- 1/2 cup (50g) cornstarch
- 1 tsp baking powder
- 1/2 tsp salt
- 1 cup (240ml) warm water
- 2 large eggs
- 1/4 cup (50g) sugar
- 1/4 cup (60ml) milk
- 2 cups (480ml) vegetable oil (for frying)

Instructions:

1. In a bowl, mix flour, cornstarch, baking powder, and salt.
2. In another bowl, whisk together eggs, sugar, milk, and water.
3. Gradually add the wet ingredients to the dry mixture until a dough forms.
4. Heat oil in a pan over medium heat.
5. Roll the dough into small balls and fry until golden brown, about 3-4 minutes. Drain on paper towels and dust with sugar.

Pan de Yuca (Yuca Bread)

Ingredients:

- 2 cups (250g) yuca flour (cassava flour)
- 1 1/2 cups (150g) grated cheese (preferably mozzarella)
- 1/2 cup (120ml) milk
- 1/4 cup (50g) unsalted butter, melted
- 2 large eggs
- 1/4 tsp salt

Instructions:

1. Preheat oven to 375°F (190°C) and grease a baking sheet.
2. In a bowl, combine yuca flour, grated cheese, and salt.
3. Add milk, melted butter, and eggs, and mix until dough forms.
4. Shape the dough into small balls and place them on the baking sheet.
5. Bake for 15-20 minutes, until golden and puffed.

Pan de Bono de Queso (Cheese Bread)

Ingredients:

- 2 cups (250g) tapioca flour
- 1 1/2 cups (150g) grated cheese (queso fresco or mozzarella)
- 1/2 cup (120ml) milk
- 1/4 cup (50g) unsalted butter, softened
- 2 large eggs
- 1/4 tsp salt

Instructions:

1. Preheat oven to 375°F (190°C) and grease a baking sheet.
2. In a bowl, combine tapioca flour, grated cheese, and salt.
3. Add milk, butter, and eggs, and mix until dough forms.
4. Shape the dough into small balls and place on the baking sheet.
5. Bake for 12-15 minutes, until golden and puffed.

Obleas

Ingredients:

- 1 package oblea wafers (available at Latin food markets)
- 1 jar (about 1 cup) of arequipe (dulce de leche) or other spreadable filling

Instructions:

1. Spread a generous amount of arequipe (or other filling) between two oblea wafers.
2. Press gently to form a sandwich.
3. Serve immediately or refrigerate until ready to serve.

Galletas de Anís (Anise Cookies)

Ingredients:

- 2 cups (250g) all-purpose flour
- 1/2 tsp baking powder
- 1/4 tsp salt
- 1 tsp ground anise seed
- 1/2 cup (115g) unsalted butter, softened
- 1/2 cup (100g) granulated sugar
- 1 large egg
- 1 tsp vanilla extract

Instructions:

1. Preheat oven to 350°F (175°C) and line a baking sheet with parchment paper.
2. Beat butter and sugar until smooth. Add vanilla extract and salt.
3. Gradually add flour and anise seeds, mixing until smooth.
4. Roll dough into small balls, place on the baking sheet, and flatten with a fork.
5. Bake for 10-12 minutes until golden and fragrant.

Galletas de Maíz (Corn Cookies)

Ingredients:

- 1 1/2 cups (190g) all-purpose flour
- 1/2 cup (60g) cornmeal
- 1/2 tsp baking powder
- 1/4 tsp salt
- 1/2 cup (115g) unsalted butter, softened
- 1/2 cup (100g) granulated sugar
- 1 large egg
- 1 tsp vanilla extract

Instructions:

1. Preheat oven to 350°F (175°C) and line a baking sheet with parchment paper.
2. In a bowl, mix together flour, cornmeal, baking powder, and salt.
3. Beat butter and sugar until light and fluffy, then add egg and vanilla extract.
4. Gradually add dry ingredients and mix until combined.
5. Roll dough into small balls, place them on the baking sheet, and flatten slightly with a fork.
6. Bake for 10-12 minutes, or until lightly golden around the edges. Let cool before serving.

Torta de Aceite (Olive Oil Cake)

Ingredients:

- 1 1/2 cups (190g) all-purpose flour
- 1 1/2 tsp baking powder
- 1/4 tsp salt
- 1 cup (240ml) olive oil
- 1 cup (200g) granulated sugar
- 3 large eggs
- 1 tsp vanilla extract
- Zest of 1 lemon (optional)

Instructions:

1. Preheat oven to 350°F (175°C) and grease a cake pan.
2. In a bowl, whisk together flour, baking powder, and salt.
3. In another bowl, beat olive oil and sugar until combined. Add eggs, one at a time, then vanilla extract and lemon zest (if using).
4. Gradually add dry ingredients to wet ingredients, mixing until smooth.
5. Pour batter into the prepared pan and bake for 30-35 minutes, or until a toothpick comes out clean. Let cool before serving.

Torta de Queso (Cheese Cake)

Ingredients:

For the crust:

- 1 1/2 cups (180g) graham cracker crumbs
- 1/4 cup (50g) granulated sugar
- 1/2 cup (115g) unsalted butter, melted

For the filling:

- 3 cups (750g) cream cheese, softened
- 1 cup (200g) granulated sugar
- 3 large eggs
- 1 tsp vanilla extract
- 1/4 cup (60ml) heavy cream

Instructions:

1. Preheat oven to 350°F (175°C) and grease a springform pan.
2. For the crust: Mix graham cracker crumbs, sugar, and melted butter. Press into the bottom of the pan.
3. For the filling: Beat cream cheese and sugar until smooth. Add eggs one at a time, then vanilla and cream.
4. Pour the filling over the crust and bake for 45-50 minutes until the center is set. Let cool, then refrigerate for 3-4 hours before serving.

Cuca (Traditional Fruit Cake)

Ingredients:

- 2 cups (250g) all-purpose flour
- 1 1/2 tsp baking powder
- 1/4 tsp salt
- 1 cup (200g) brown sugar
- 1/2 cup (120ml) vegetable oil
- 2 large eggs
- 1 tsp vanilla extract
- 1 1/2 cups (200g) mixed dried fruits (raisins, currants, etc.)
- 1/2 tsp ground cinnamon
- 1/4 tsp ground nutmeg

Instructions:

1. Preheat oven to 350°F (175°C) and grease a loaf pan.
2. In a bowl, whisk together flour, baking powder, and salt.
3. In another bowl, beat oil and brown sugar until smooth. Add eggs, one at a time, then vanilla extract.
4. Gradually add dry ingredients, alternating with milk, and mix until smooth.
5. Fold in dried fruits.
6. Pour the batter into the pan and bake for 45-50 minutes until a toothpick comes out clean. Let cool before serving.

Bizcochos (Biscuits)

Ingredients:

- 2 cups (250g) all-purpose flour
- 1 tsp baking powder
- 1/4 tsp salt
- 1/2 cup (115g) unsalted butter, chilled and cubed
- 1/4 cup (50g) granulated sugar
- 1 large egg
- 1/4 cup (60ml) milk

Instructions:

1. Preheat oven to 375°F (190°C) and line a baking sheet with parchment paper.
2. In a bowl, combine flour, baking powder, and salt.
3. Cut in the butter until the mixture resembles coarse crumbs.
4. Beat the egg and stir it into the mixture, followed by the milk.
5. Drop spoonfuls of dough onto the baking sheet and bake for 10-12 minutes until golden.

Torta de Naranja (Orange Cake)

Ingredients:

- 2 cups (250g) all-purpose flour
- 1 1/2 tsp baking powder
- 1/4 tsp salt
- 1 cup (240ml) fresh orange juice
- Zest of 2 oranges
- 1 cup (200g) granulated sugar
- 1/2 cup (115g) unsalted butter, softened
- 3 large eggs

Instructions:

1. Preheat oven to 350°F (175°C) and grease a cake pan.
2. In a bowl, whisk together flour, baking powder, and salt.
3. In another bowl, beat butter and sugar until creamy. Add eggs, one at a time, then vanilla extract and pureed pumpkin.
4. Gradually add dry ingredients and mix until smooth.
5. Pour the batter into the pan and bake for 30-35 minutes, or until golden. Let cool before serving.

Roscones (Sweet Buns)

Ingredients:

- 2 cups (250g) all-purpose flour
- 1/4 cup (50g) granulated sugar
- 1 packet (7g) active dry yeast
- 1/2 tsp salt
- 1/2 cup (120ml) warm milk
- 1/4 cup (60g) unsalted butter, softened
- 1 large egg
- 1/2 tsp vanilla extract

Instructions:

1. Preheat oven to 350°F (175°C) and grease a baking sheet.
2. In a bowl, dissolve yeast and sugar in warm milk and let sit for 5-10 minutes.
3. In another bowl, mix flour and salt. Add the yeast mixture, butter, egg, and vanilla. Knead until smooth.
4. Let the dough rise for 1 hour, then shape into rounds or rings.
5. Place on the baking sheet, let rise for another 20 minutes, and bake for 15-20 minutes until golden.

Pan de Leche (Milk Bread)

Ingredients:

- 2 cups (250g) all-purpose flour
- 1 packet (7g) active dry yeast
- 1/4 cup (50g) granulated sugar
- 1/2 tsp salt
- 3/4 cup (180ml) whole milk
- 1/4 cup (60g) unsalted butter, softened
- 1 large egg

Instructions:

1. Dissolve sugar and yeast in warm milk and let sit for 5-10 minutes.
2. In a bowl, combine flour and salt, then add the yeast mixture, butter, and egg. Knead until smooth.
3. Let dough rise for 1-1.5 hours, then shape into a loaf and place in a greased pan.
4. Let rise for 30 minutes, then bake at 350°F (175°C) for 25-30 minutes until golden.

Postre de Natas (Milk Pudding)

Ingredients:

- 4 cups (960ml) whole milk
- 1/2 cup (100g) granulated sugar
- 1/2 tsp vanilla extract
- 3 large egg yolks
- 2 tbsp cornstarch

Instructions:

1. In a saucepan, heat milk and sugar over medium heat until warm.
2. In a bowl, whisk together egg yolks and cornstarch until smooth.
3. Slowly add the warm milk mixture to the egg mixture, then return to the pan and cook until thickened.
4. Pour into serving dishes and let cool. Chill before serving.

Tamales

Ingredients:

For the dough:

- 2 cups (250g) masa harina
- 1 cup (240ml) chicken or vegetable broth
- 1/2 cup (115g) unsalted butter, softened
- 1 tsp baking powder
- 1/2 tsp salt

For the filling:

- 2 cups (300g) cooked shredded chicken or pork
- 1/2 cup (120g) red or green salsa

Instructions:

1. Soak corn husks in warm water for 30 minutes.
2. In a bowl, mix masa harina, broth, butter, baking powder, and salt until dough is soft and pliable.
3. Spread a portion of the dough onto a corn husk, add a spoonful of filling, and fold the husk.
4. Steam tamales for 1-1.5 hours until the dough is fully cooked.

Churros

Ingredients:

- 1 cup (240ml) water
- 2 tbsp granulated sugar
- 1/4 tsp salt
- 2 tbsp unsalted butter
- 1 cup (125g) all-purpose flour
- 2 large eggs
- 2 cups (480ml) vegetable oil (for frying)
- 1/2 cup (100g) granulated sugar (for coating)
- 1 tsp ground cinnamon (optional)

Instructions:

1. In a saucepan, bring water, sugar, salt, and butter to a boil.
2. Stir in flour until a dough forms.
3. Remove from heat, add eggs one at a time, and mix until smooth.
4. Heat oil in a pan to 375°F (190°C).
5. Pipe the dough into the hot oil in long strips, frying until golden and crispy.
6. Coat with a mixture of sugar and cinnamon.

Torta de Chocolate (Chocolate Cake)

Ingredients:

- 2 cups (250g) all-purpose flour
- 1 1/2 tsp baking powder
- 1/2 tsp baking soda
- 1/4 tsp salt
- 1 cup (200g) granulated sugar
- 1/2 cup (115g) unsalted butter, softened
- 2 large eggs
- 1 tsp vanilla extract
- 1 cup (240ml) whole milk
- 1/2 cup (50g) unsweetened cocoa powder

Instructions:

1. Preheat oven to 350°F (175°C) and grease a round cake pan.
2. In a bowl, whisk together flour, baking powder, baking soda, salt, and cocoa powder.
3. Beat butter and sugar until fluffy. Add eggs one at a time, then vanilla extract.
4. Gradually add dry ingredients, alternating with milk, mixing until smooth.
5. Pour batter into the prepared pan and bake for 30-35 minutes until a toothpick comes out clean. Let cool before serving.

Galletas de Coco (Coconut Cookies)

Ingredients:

- 1 1/2 cups (180g) shredded coconut
- 1 cup (125g) all-purpose flour
- 1/2 cup (100g) granulated sugar
- 1/2 cup (115g) unsalted butter, softened
- 1 large egg
- 1 tsp vanilla extract
- 1/2 tsp baking powder

Instructions:

1. Preheat oven to 350°F (175°C) and line a baking sheet with parchment paper.
2. Beat butter and sugar until light and fluffy, then add egg and vanilla extract.
3. Stir in shredded coconut, flour, and baking powder until well combined.
4. Drop spoonfuls of dough onto the baking sheet.
5. Bake for 10-12 minutes until golden. Let cool before serving.

Merengones (Large Meringues)

Ingredients:

- 4 large egg whites
- 1 cup (200g) granulated sugar
- 1 tsp vanilla extract
- 1/4 tsp cream of tartar

Instructions:

1. Preheat oven to 250°F (120°C) and line a baking sheet with parchment paper.
2. Beat egg whites and cream of tartar until soft peaks form. Gradually add sugar, one tablespoon at a time, and continue beating until stiff peaks form.
3. Stir in vanilla extract.
4. Spoon or pipe the meringue mixture onto the baking sheet into large mounds.
5. Bake for 1.5-2 hours until dry and crisp. Let cool completely before serving.

Chocoramo (Chocolate Coated Cake)

Ingredients:

For the cake:

- 1 1/2 cups (190g) all-purpose flour
- 1 1/2 tsp baking powder
- 1/4 tsp salt
- 1/2 cup (100g) granulated sugar
- 1/2 cup (120ml) milk
- 1/2 cup (115g) unsalted butter, softened
- 2 large eggs
- 1 tsp vanilla extract

For the chocolate coating:

- 1 cup (170g) semisweet chocolate, chopped
- 2 tbsp unsalted butter

Instructions:

1. Preheat oven to 350°F (175°C) and grease a loaf pan.
2. In a bowl, whisk together flour, baking powder, and salt.
3. Beat butter and sugar until fluffy. Add eggs one at a time, then vanilla extract.
4. Gradually add dry ingredients, alternating with milk, mixing until smooth.
5. Pour batter into the pan and bake for 30-35 minutes, until a toothpick comes out clean. Let cool.
6. For the chocolate coating: Melt chocolate and butter in a saucepan.
7. Dip the cooled cake into the chocolate coating or drizzle it over the top. Let it set before serving.

Pionono

Ingredients:

- 1 cup (125g) all-purpose flour
- 1/2 tsp baking powder
- 1/4 tsp salt
- 1/2 cup (100g) granulated sugar
- 4 large eggs
- 1 tsp vanilla extract
- 1/2 cup (120ml) whipped cream or chocolate ganache for filling

Instructions:

1. Preheat oven to 350°F (175°C) and line a jelly roll pan with parchment paper.
2. Beat eggs and sugar until thick and fluffy, then add vanilla extract.
3. Gradually fold in flour, baking powder, and salt.
4. Pour the batter into the prepared pan and bake for 10-12 minutes until golden.
5. Turn the cake out onto a clean towel and roll it up while warm. Let cool slightly.
6. Unroll the cake, spread whipped cream or ganache, and roll back up. Slice and serve.

Cocadas

Ingredients:

- 2 cups (240g) shredded coconut
- 1/2 cup (100g) granulated sugar
- 1/4 cup (60ml) water
- 1/2 tsp vanilla extract

Instructions:

1. Preheat oven to 350°F (175°C) and line a baking sheet with parchment paper.
2. In a saucepan, melt sugar and water over medium heat until sugar dissolves.
3. Stir in shredded coconut and vanilla extract.
4. Drop spoonfuls of the mixture onto the baking sheet.
5. Bake for 10-12 minutes until golden and set. Let cool before serving.

Masarepa con Queso (Arepa with Cheese)

Ingredients:

- 2 cups (250g) masarepa (pre-cooked cornmeal)
- 1 1/2 cups (360ml) warm water
- 1 tsp salt
- 1/2 cup (115g) grated cheese (mozzarella or queso fresco)
- 1 tbsp butter (optional)

Instructions:

1. In a bowl, combine masarepa, warm water, and salt. Mix until smooth and doughy.
2. Stir in grated cheese and butter, if using.
3. Form the dough into small patties or rounds.
4. Heat a pan over medium heat and cook the arepas for 3-4 minutes on each side until golden.

Pasteles de Carne (Meat Patties)

Ingredients:

For the dough:

- 2 cups (250g) all-purpose flour
- 1/2 tsp salt
- 1/2 cup (120g) unsalted butter, chilled and cubed
- 1 egg
- 1/4 cup (60ml) cold water

For the filling:

- 1 lb (450g) ground beef or pork
- 1 small onion, chopped
- 1/2 cup (75g) diced potatoes (optional)
- 1/4 cup (60ml) tomato sauce
- 1 tsp cumin
- 1/4 tsp paprika
- Salt and pepper to taste

Instructions:

1. For the dough: In a bowl, mix flour and salt. Add butter and rub into the flour until crumbly.
2. Add egg and water and mix until dough forms. Cover and refrigerate for 30 minutes.
3. For the filling: Cook ground meat with onions and spices. Add tomato sauce and potatoes, if using, and cook until well combined. Let cool.
4. Roll out dough, cut into circles, and spoon the filling into the center. Fold and seal the edges.
5. Fry in hot oil for 3-4 minutes until golden, or bake at 375°F (190°C) for 20 minutes.

Canelazos

Ingredients:

- 4 cups (960ml) water
- 1/2 cup (100g) sugar
- 2 cinnamon sticks
- 1/2 cup (120ml) aguardiente or rum (optional)

Instructions:

1. In a saucepan, combine water, sugar, and cinnamon sticks.
2. Bring to a boil, then reduce heat and simmer for 10-15 minutes to infuse the flavors.
3. Add aguardiente or rum, if desired, and stir.
4. Serve hot in mugs.

Empanaditas de Dulce (Sweet Empanadas)

Ingredients:

For the dough:

- 2 cups (250g) all-purpose flour
- 1/4 cup (50g) granulated sugar
- 1/2 cup (115g) unsalted butter, softened
- 1 large egg
- 1/4 cup (60ml) milk

For the filling:

- 1/2 cup (100g) sweetened fruit jam (e.g., guava or quince)

Instructions:

1. Preheat oven to 350°F (175°C) and line a baking sheet with parchment paper.
2. For the dough: Mix flour, sugar, and butter until crumbly. Add egg and milk, mixing until dough forms.
3. Roll dough out and cut into small rounds.
4. Place a small spoonful of fruit jam in the center of each round, then fold and seal the edges.
5. Bake for 12-15 minutes, until golden.

Torta de Arándano (Blueberry Cake)

Ingredients:

- 2 cups (250g) all-purpose flour
- 1 1/2 tsp baking powder
- 1/4 tsp salt
- 1 cup (200g) granulated sugar
- 1/2 cup (115g) unsalted butter, softened
- 2 large eggs
- 1 tsp vanilla extract
- 1 cup (150g) fresh blueberries

Instructions:

1. Preheat oven to 350°F (175°C) and grease a round cake pan.
2. In a bowl, whisk together flour, baking powder, and salt.
3. Beat butter and sugar until fluffy, then add eggs one at a time, followed by vanilla extract.
4. Gradually add dry ingredients, mixing until smooth.
5. Gently fold in blueberries.
6. Pour batter into the pan and bake for 30-35 minutes, or until golden. Let cool before serving.

Galletas de Guanábana (Soursop Cookies)

Ingredients:

- 1 cup (240g) guanábana pulp (fresh or frozen)
- 1/2 cup (100g) granulated sugar
- 1 cup (125g) graham cracker crumbs
- 1/4 cup (60g) unsalted butter, melted
- 1/2 cup (60g) sweetened condensed milk
- 1/2 tsp vanilla extract

Instructions:

1. In a bowl, mix the guanábana pulp, sugar, graham cracker crumbs, melted butter, sweetened condensed milk, and vanilla extract until combined.
2. Shape the mixture into small bite-sized balls or press into a lined baking pan.
3. Chill in the refrigerator for 2-3 hours until firm.
4. Serve chilled, optionally dusted with a little powdered sugar.

Pan de Piña (Pineapple Bread)

Ingredients:

- 2 cups (250g) all-purpose flour
- 1 1/2 tsp baking powder
- 1/4 tsp salt
- 1 cup (240ml) pineapple juice
- 1/2 cup (115g) unsalted butter, softened
- 1 cup (200g) granulated sugar
- 2 large eggs
- 1 tsp vanilla extract
- 1/2 cup (120g) crushed pineapple (drained)

Instructions:

1. Preheat oven to 350°F (175°C) and grease a loaf pan.
2. In a bowl, whisk together flour, baking powder, and salt.
3. In another bowl, beat butter and sugar until smooth. Add eggs one at a time, then vanilla extract.
4. Gradually mix in the dry ingredients, alternating with pineapple juice. Stir in crushed pineapple.
5. Pour the batter into the pan and bake for 45-50 minutes, or until a toothpick comes out clean. Let cool before serving.

Bizcocho de Tres Leches (Three Milk Cake)

Ingredients:

For the cake:

- 1 1/2 cups (190g) all-purpose flour
- 1 1/2 tsp baking powder
- 1/4 tsp salt
- 1 cup (200g) granulated sugar
- 5 large eggs
- 1 tsp vanilla extract
- 1/2 cup (120ml) whole milk

For the milk mixture:

- 1 cup (240ml) whole milk
- 1/2 cup (120ml) evaporated milk
- 1/2 cup (120ml) sweetened condensed milk

For the topping:

- 1 cup (240ml) heavy cream
- 2 tbsp powdered sugar

Instructions:

1. Preheat oven to 350°F (175°C) and grease a round cake pan.
2. For the cake: Beat eggs and sugar until thick and pale. Add vanilla extract.
3. Gradually fold in flour, baking powder, and salt. Add milk and mix until smooth.
4. Pour the batter into the pan and bake for 25-30 minutes until a toothpick comes out clean.
5. For the milk mixture: In a bowl, combine all the milk ingredients.
6. Once the cake is baked and cooled slightly, poke holes in it with a fork and pour the milk mixture over the cake. Let the cake absorb the milk for at least an hour.
7. For the topping: Whip the heavy cream with powdered sugar until stiff. Spread over the cake before serving.

Arroz con Leche (Rice Pudding)

Ingredients:

- 1 cup (200g) short-grain rice
- 4 cups (960ml) whole milk
- 1/2 cup (100g) granulated sugar
- 1/4 tsp salt
- 1 tsp ground cinnamon
- 1/2 tsp vanilla extract

Instructions:

1. Rinse the rice under cold water.
2. In a large pot, combine rice, milk, sugar, and salt. Bring to a simmer over medium heat.
3. Stir occasionally and cook for 30-40 minutes until the rice is tender and the mixture thickens.
4. Remove from heat and stir in cinnamon and vanilla extract.
5. Serve warm or chilled, garnished with additional cinnamon if desired.

Panqueques con Arequipe (Pancakes with Dulce de Leche)

Ingredients:

For the pancakes:

- 1 1/2 cups (190g) all-purpose flour
- 1 tbsp sugar
- 1 tsp baking powder
- 1/2 tsp salt
- 1 1/4 cups (300ml) milk
- 1 large egg
- 2 tbsp unsalted butter, melted

For the topping:

- 1/2 cup (120g) arequipe (dulce de leche)

Instructions:

1. Preheat a griddle or frying pan over medium heat.
2. In a bowl, whisk together flour, sugar, baking powder, and salt.
3. In another bowl, whisk together milk, egg, and melted butter.
4. Add wet ingredients to dry ingredients and stir until smooth.
5. Pour batter onto the griddle to form pancakes. Cook for 2-3 minutes on each side.
6. Drizzle warm arequipe over the pancakes before serving.

Ajiaco (Served with Bread)

Ingredients:

- 2 lbs (900g) chicken breast
- 1 lb (450g) potatoes, peeled and chopped
- 1/2 cup (120g) corn kernels (fresh or frozen)
- 2 cups (480ml) chicken broth
- 1 small onion, chopped
- 2 cloves garlic, minced
- 1 tsp cumin
- 1/4 tsp black pepper
- 1 tbsp fresh cilantro, chopped
- Salt to taste
- Bread (for serving)

Instructions:

1. In a large pot, combine chicken, potatoes, corn, chicken broth, onion, garlic, cumin, and black pepper.
2. Bring to a boil, then reduce heat and simmer for 30-40 minutes, until the potatoes are tender and the chicken is cooked through.
3. Shred the chicken in the pot, then stir in cilantro and salt to taste.
4. Serve the soup hot with bread on the side.

Pan Relleno de Dulce (Sweet Filled Bread)

Ingredients:

For the dough:

- 2 cups (250g) all-purpose flour
- 1/2 tsp salt
- 1/4 cup (50g) granulated sugar
- 1 packet (7g) active dry yeast
- 1/4 cup (60ml) warm water
- 1/4 cup (60g) unsalted butter, softened
- 1 large egg

For the filling:

- 1/2 cup (100g) fruit jam or dulce de leche

Instructions:

1. In a bowl, dissolve yeast and sugar in warm water and let sit for 5-10 minutes.
2. Add flour, salt, butter, and egg to the yeast mixture. Knead until smooth and elastic.
3. Let dough rise for 1 hour until doubled in size.
4. Roll out dough and spread fruit jam or dulce de leche in the center. Roll up the dough and shape into a loaf.
5. Let rise for 30 minutes, then bake at 350°F (175°C) for 20-25 minutes until golden. Let cool before serving.

Pargo Frito con Yuca (Fried Snapper with Cassava)

Ingredients:

- 2 whole snapper fish, cleaned and gutted
- 1 tbsp garlic powder
- 1 tbsp paprika
- 1/2 tsp salt
- 1/2 tsp black pepper
- 2 cups (480ml) vegetable oil (for frying)
- 2 cups (300g) yuca, peeled and boiled until soft

Instructions:

1. Season the fish with garlic powder, paprika, salt, and pepper.
2. Heat oil in a large pan over medium heat. Fry the fish for 4-5 minutes on each side until golden and crispy.
3. Serve the fried fish with boiled yuca on the side.

Torta de Maíz (Corn Cake)

Ingredients:

- 2 cups (250g) cornmeal
- 1/2 cup (100g) sugar
- 1/2 tsp baking powder
- 1/4 tsp salt
- 2 cups (480ml) milk
- 1/4 cup (60g) unsalted butter, melted
- 2 large eggs

Instructions:

1. Preheat oven to 350°F (175°C) and grease a cake pan.
2. In a bowl, mix together cornmeal, sugar, baking powder, and salt.
3. In another bowl, whisk together milk, melted butter, and eggs.
4. Gradually add the wet ingredients to the dry ingredients, stirring until smooth.
5. Pour the batter into the prepared pan and bake for 25-30 minutes, or until golden. Let cool before serving.

Mazamorra (Corn Pudding)

Ingredients:

- 1 1/2 cups (180g) dried hominy corn
- 1 1/2 cups (300g) sugar
- 4 cups (960ml) water
- 1/2 tsp cinnamon

Instructions:

1. Rinse the hominy corn and soak it in water overnight.
2. In a large pot, bring water to a boil. Add soaked hominy and simmer for 1-1.5 hours until tender.
3. Add sugar and cinnamon, then cook for another 20 minutes.
4. Serve hot or chilled, topped with extra cinnamon or sugar if desired.

Dulce de Leche

Ingredients:

- 4 cups (960ml) whole milk
- 2 cups (400g) granulated sugar
- 1/4 tsp baking soda

Instructions:

1. In a large saucepan, combine milk, sugar, and baking soda.
2. Bring to a simmer over medium heat, stirring frequently.
3. Reduce the heat and cook for 1.5-2 hours, stirring occasionally, until it thickens to a caramel-like consistency.
4. Let it cool before transferring to jars.

Bocaditos de Guanábana (Soursop Bites)

Ingredients:

- 1 cup (240g) guanábana pulp (fresh or frozen)
- 1/2 cup (100g) granulated sugar
- 1 cup (125g) graham cracker crumbs
- 1/4 cup (60g) unsalted butter, melted
- 1/2 cup (60g) sweetened condensed milk
- 1/2 tsp vanilla extract

Instructions:

1. In a bowl, mix the guanábana pulp, sugar, graham cracker crumbs, melted butter, sweetened condensed milk, and vanilla extract until combined.
2. Shape the mixture into small bite-sized balls or press into a lined baking pan.
3. Chill in the refrigerator for 2-3 hours until firm.
4. Serve chilled, optionally dusted with a little powdered sugar.

Torta de Remolacha (Beet Cake)

Ingredients:

- 2 cups (250g) all-purpose flour
- 1 1/2 tsp baking powder
- 1/4 tsp baking soda
- 1/4 tsp salt
- 1 cup (200g) granulated sugar
- 1/2 cup (120ml) vegetable oil
- 2 large eggs
- 1 tsp vanilla extract
- 1 1/2 cups (225g) cooked and pureed beets

For the frosting:

- 1 cup (240g) cream cheese, softened
- 1/2 cup (115g) unsalted butter, softened
- 2 cups (250g) powdered sugar
- 1 tsp vanilla extract

Instructions:

1. Preheat oven to 350°F (175°C) and grease a cake pan.
2. In a bowl, whisk together flour, baking powder, baking soda, and salt.
3. In another bowl, beat sugar and oil together until smooth. Add eggs one at a time, then vanilla extract.
4. Stir in the pureed beets. Gradually add the dry ingredients and mix until smooth.
5. Pour the batter into the pan and bake for 30-35 minutes, or until a toothpick comes out clean. Let cool.
6. For the frosting: Beat cream cheese and butter until smooth. Gradually add powdered sugar and vanilla extract.
7. Frost the cooled cake and serve.

Suspiros (Meringue Cookies)

Ingredients:

- 4 large egg whites
- 1 cup (200g) granulated sugar
- 1 tsp vanilla extract
- 1/4 tsp cream of tartar

Instructions:

1. Preheat oven to 250°F (120°C) and line a baking sheet with parchment paper.
2. Beat egg whites and cream of tartar until soft peaks form. Gradually add sugar, one tablespoon at a time, and continue beating until stiff peaks form.
3. Stir in vanilla extract.
4. Spoon or pipe the meringue onto the baking sheet in small rounds.
5. Bake for 1.5-2 hours until dry and crisp. Let cool completely before serving.

Pan de Zapallo (Pumpkin Bread)

Ingredients:

- 2 cups (250g) all-purpose flour
- 1 1/2 tsp baking powder
- 1/2 tsp baking soda
- 1/4 tsp salt
- 1 tsp ground cinnamon
- 1/2 tsp ground nutmeg
- 1 1/2 cups (350g) pureed pumpkin
- 1/2 cup (115g) unsalted butter, softened
- 1 cup (200g) granulated sugar
- 2 large eggs
- 1 tsp vanilla extract

Instructions:

1. Preheat oven to 350°F (175°C) and grease a loaf pan.
2. In a bowl, whisk together flour, baking powder, baking soda, salt, cinnamon, and nutmeg.
3. In another bowl, beat butter and sugar until light and fluffy. Add eggs one at a time, then vanilla extract and pureed pumpkin.
4. Gradually add the dry ingredients and mix until smooth.
5. Pour the batter into the pan and bake for 50-60 minutes, or until a toothpick comes out clean. Let cool before serving.

Pudding de Aguacate (Avocado Pudding)

Ingredients:

- 2 ripe avocados, peeled and pitted
- 1/2 cup (120ml) milk (or coconut milk for a dairy-free option)
- 1/4 cup (50g) granulated sugar
- 1 tsp vanilla extract
- A pinch of salt

Instructions:

1. In a blender, combine avocados, milk, sugar, vanilla extract, and salt. Blend until smooth and creamy.
2. Taste and adjust sweetness by adding more sugar, if necessary.
3. Pour the pudding into serving glasses and refrigerate for 2-3 hours until chilled.
4. Serve topped with fresh fruit or a drizzle of honey if desired.

Brevas con Arequipe (Figs with Dulce de Leche)

Ingredients:

- 8-10 ripe figs, halved
- 1/2 cup (120g) arequipe (dulce de leche)

Instructions:

1. Slice figs in half, removing the stems if necessary.
2. Spoon a small amount of arequipe onto the center of each fig half.
3. Arrange the figs on a serving platter and serve immediately. Alternatively, chill for 30 minutes for a cool dessert.

www.ingramcontent.com/pod-product-compliance
Lightning Source LLC
LaVergne TN
LVHW081340060526
838201LV00055B/2765